Excel

BASIC SKILLS
HOMEWORK BOOK

GRAMMAR AND PUNCTUATION

BOOK 1

YEARS 3–4

PETER M. CLUTTERBUCK

PASCAL
PRESS

Pascal Press
PO Box 250
Glebe NSW 2037
(02) 8585 4044
www.pascalpress.com.au

Typeset by Grizzly Graphics
Cover by Dizign
Printed in Singapore by Green Giant Press

About this book…

The Basic Skills Support Books are designed to help children increase their word knowledge and general language skills. Students are introduced to simple grammatical terms and punctuation marks through activities that present them in context.

Through the mastery tests provided, parents and teachers are easily able to locate areas where difficulty is being experienced and then guide the child to the appropriate activities to assist him or her.

These books contain all the elements of grammar and punctuation relevant to children aged 8-10.

GRAMMAR AND PUNCTUATION YEARS 3 + 4
TABLE OF CONTENTS

The vowels are *a, e, i, o* and *u*.

We use ***an*** in front of words that begin with vowels.
For example, ***an*** *ice-cream,* ***an*** *apple.*

We use ***a*** before words that begin with the other letters.
For example, ***a*** *dog,* ***a*** *pig.*

Use *a* or *an* in the spaces.

1. I ate _____ apple and _____ banana.

2. Tom found _____ egg and _____ axe in the bush.

3. Sally brought _____ dog and _____ kitten to school.

4. The old doll only has _____ arm and _____ leg left on the body.

5. In the boat was _____ oar and _____ sail.

6. A bee is _____ insect and a magpie is _____ bird.

7. In our kitchen is _____ oven and _____ heater.

8. In the jungle was _____ ostrich and _____ elephant.

9. Six is _____ even number and nine is _____ odd number.

10. I have _____ young dog but Paul has _____ old dog.

A *noun* is a naming word. It can be used to name a person, place, thing or feeling.

Example Which word best fills the gap?
A _____ can lay an egg.
*Answer = **hen**. A **hen** can lay an egg.*

Now do these.

1. A _____ can bark.
   (a) frog   (b) dog   (c) log

2. My brother can drive a _____.
   (a) car   (b) star   (c) far

3. I ride my _____ to school.
   (a) baby   (b) hike   (c) bike

4. A _____ will open a door.
   (a) flea   (b) key   (c) tea

5. My _____ has a long tail.
   (a) cat   (b) hat   (c) shoe

6. I like to eat _____.
   (a) cake   (b) lake   (c) tree

7. A _____ has a fluffy tail.
   (a) habit   (b) fly   (c) rabbit

8. Dogs like to chew _____.
   (a) stones   (b) cones   (c) bones

9. Circle the nouns in the following passage:

   Mum, Dad, Ned and Freya were going to the zoo. They caught the bus into town, the ferry across the harbour and the cablecar to the entrance of the zoo. "I want to see the monkeys," cried Freya. "I want to look at the tigers," shouted Ned. "I want to sit down and have a rest," said Mum, even though it wasn't even lunchtime yet. "Not yet," said Dad. "We'll let our little animals see some of the zoo's big animals first, then we'll sit under that tree and have some food."

Remember, a *noun* is simply the name of something.

Example   *What name am I?*
I have four legs. You can sit on me. I am often near a table. I am a _____.
*Answer = **chair**.*

Choose a word from the box to complete this quiz.

frog	star	bee	car
cow	egg	fire	shoe

1. I am high up in the sky.
   I twinkle at night.
   I am a _____.

2. I have a shell.
   I am yellow and white inside.
   Birds lay me.
   I am an _____.

3. I am small and have wings.
   I gather nectar from flowers.
   I use it to make honey.
   I am a _____.

4. I am made of leather.
   I have laces.
   I am worn on the foot.
   I am a _____.

5. I have horns.
   I eat grass.
   I give milk.
   I am a _____.

6. I live near water.
   Sometimes I am green.
   I croak.
   I am a _____.

7. I have wheels and doors.
   Inside I have seats.
   I take people places.
   I am a _____.

8. I am red and very hot.
   I can burn wood.
   You should never touch me.
   I am a _____.

Nouns are used to name animals, plants and things that we make or use.

Example   Circle the words which are the names of animals.

paper   bear   lion   horse   table

Answer is   (bear)   (lion)   (horse)

Now do these.

1. Circle the words that are the names of birds.

    teapot magpie emu cow eagle

2. Circle the words that are the names of fruit.

    apple apricot potato plum truck

3. Circle the words that are the names of furniture.

    donkey desk chair orange table

4. Circle the words that are the names of flowers.

    rose daffodil violet lion tree

5. Circle the words that are the names of drinks.

    crow milk soda bucket cola

6. Circle the words that are the names of food.

    cake tart meat girl page

7. Circle the words that are the names of insects.

    fish fly moth glass butterfly

8. Circle the words that are the names of footwear.

    grass mat shoe sandal slippers

9. Circle the words that are the names of things we wear.

    bee tie tadpole shirt dress

10. Circle the words that are the names of things that can fly.

    kite plane airship car bottle

Some nouns are used to name collections of people or things. These are called *collective nouns.*

Example Which word best fills the gap?
I saw a _____ of birds.
gang   flock   bunch
*Answer = **flock***

Choose the word that best fills the gap.

1. The farmer had a large _____ of sheep.

   crew   swarm   flock

2. The _____ of angry bees chased Billy.

   bunch   swarm   herd

3. The _____ of netballers was on the court.

   team   box   bundle

4. I ate a whole _____ of grapes.

   flock   fleet   bunch

5. The _____ of cows is in the yard.

   herd   crew   flight

6. A _____ of ships is in the harbour.

   bunch   fleet   flock

7. Our dog had a _____ of puppies.

   bunch   class   litter

8. We walked through the _____ of trees.

   box   forest   bundle

9. I threw the _____ of rags into the box.

   bundle   swarm   flock

10. I bought a _____ of biscuits.

    class   team   packet

Some nouns must be written with a capital letter because they name a person or place. The names of your friends, the days of the weeks, the months of the year, and the names of towns, countries and cities, always begin with a capital letter.

Example

Which word should begin with a capital letter?

book   *peter*   *water*

Answer = (*Peter*)

Circle the word in each group that should begin with a capital.
Write the word with a capital.

1. lamp   monday   bone

   _____

2. feet   soil   susan

   _____

3. april   boat   brush

   _____

4. water   fish   friday

   _____

5. melbourne   knife   spoon

   _____

6. katy   father   jelly

   _____

7. september   note   clothes

   _____

8. cord   england   chair

   _____

9. Write the names of your three best friends.

   _____   _____   _____

10. Write the name of your teacher. _____

11. Write the name of the street in which you live. _____

12. Write out the month in which your birthday is. _____

Here are some more questions on proper nouns.

Example

Colour the boxes that contain the names of people blue.
Colour the boxes that contain the names of months or days red.
Colour the boxes that contain the names of places green.

Albania	Joshua	Tuesday	Lithgow	Friday
July	Africa	Gina	Grandad	Wendy
Mrs Smith	August	Paris	Sunday	June
December	Fiji	Michelle	Mr Jones	Newcastle

Look at these days of the week.

Sunday Monday Tuesday Wednesday Thursday Friday Saturday

1. Write the days you do not come to school. _____ _____

2. Write the first school day of each week. _____

3. Write the last school day of each week. _____

4. Write the middle day of the week. _____

5. What day comes after Sunday? _____

6. What day comes before Wednesday? _____

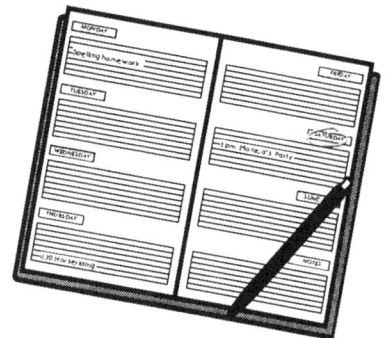

7. Write your favourite day of the week. Say why. _____

_____

Nouns can name things that are singular (one), for example, boy, cow, house.
They can also name things that are plural (more than one), for example, two *boys*,
five *cows*, lots of *houses*.

Colour the boxes that contain words that mean more than one.

book	chairs	bat
windows	table	trees
pages	birds	cup
desk	flower	roads

Now, make each word at the end of the sentence mean more than one. Write the word in the
space.

1. The farmer has three _____.
    (cow)

2. A bird laid two _____. (egg)

3. There are four _____ in the
    room. (bed)

4. Callan was given two _____.
    (toy)

5. A lot of _____ ate the
    cheese. (rat)

6. There are five _____ in our
    street. (shop)

7. All the _____ are twinkling.
    (star)

8. There are five _____ in the
    yard. (pig)

9. We bounced some _____ in
    the playground. (ball)

10. There were lots of _____ at
    the zoo. (bear)

Nouns ending in -s, -sh, -ch or -x make their plurals by adding -es.

Example   There were lots of _____ on his jeans. (patch)
         *Answer = **patches***

Write the plural of the word in brackets in the space.

1. There were six _____ growing in the garden. (bush)

2. I ate two _____ for lunch. (peach)

3. We saw six _____ in the forest. (fox)

4. There are four _____ parked in the street. (bus)

5. We put the four _____ of books on the table. (box)

6. The two _____ broke when they fell. (glass)

7. There are lots of _____ in our bathroom. (brush)

8. In this street there are three large _____. (church)

9. Our school has twenty _____. (class)

10. I put all the _____ back in the box. (match)

For nouns that end in -y, and have a vowel before the -y, simply add -s to make the plural.

For example,   *key — keys*   *holiday — holidays*

Write the plural. donkey   _____

toy   _____

Nouns that end with **-y** but have a consonant before the **-y** form their plural by changing the **-y** to **-i** and adding **-es**.

For example,   *city — cities*   *fly — flies*

Write the plural. pony   _____

baby   _____

All the words in the grid end in -y. Find the words and list them in the 'Singular' column. Write each word as a plural. One has been done for you.

t	r	a	y	s
d	k	t	b	p
a	e	o	o	r
y	y	y	y	a
b	u	o	y	y

Singular One	Plural More Than One
spray	sprays
_____	_____
_____	_____
_____	_____
_____	_____
_____	_____
_____	_____

Some words change their form for the plural.

For example,   *one woman — two women*   *one mouse — five mice*

Write the plural for these.

one foot   two _____   one tooth   lots of _____

one man   three _____   one child   two _____

Verbs are words that tell us what people, animals or things are doing.

Example

*The girl is **walking**.*
*The monkey is **climbing**.*

Choose the verb which best completes the sentence.
Write it in the space.

1. Bruno is _____ in a chair.
   (a) hitting   (b) sitting   (c) flying

2. My mother is _____ us to school in our car.
   (a) jumping (b) driving   (c) eating

3. The girls are _____ over the ropes.
   (a) crying   (b) kicking   (c) jumping

4. Tom is _____ a pie for lunch.
   (a) eating   (b) crying   (c) playing

5. Jack is _____ the ball.
   (a) writing   (b) kicking (c) heating

6. Oona is _____ a book.
   (a) catching (b) pushing   (c) reading

7. Tom is _____ a pram.
   (a) pushing (b) catching (c) hoping

8. Chan is _____ a story.
   (a) playing (b) writing (c) marrying

9. The boy is _____ up the tree.
   (a) crying   (b) climbing (c) firing

10. Renee is _____ her bicycle.
    (a) scratching (b) roasting (c) riding

Verbs are words that tell us what people, animals or things are doing.

For example,   The girl **ran**.
                  The ball **bounced**.

Circle the verb that best completes each question.
Write each complete question in the space.

For example,   Can you ((boil,) wash) some water?

                  Can you boil some water?

1. Can you (draw, ride) a picture?

    _____

2. Can you (paint, dig) a hole?

    _____

3. Can you (catch, dry) a ball?

    _____

4. Can you (fry, paint) some meat?

    _____

5. Can you (boil, write) a story?

    _____

6. Can you (bend, set) your knees?

    _____

7. Can you (fly, dig) a kite?

    _____

8. Can you (eat, dry) a pie?

    _____

9. Can you (play, stay) a game?

    _____

10. Can you (clap, help) your friend?

    _____

We must always use *is* and *are* carefully.

We use *is* when we are talking about one person or thing.
    *For example,   Jack **is** in the room.   The dog **is** in the kennel.*

We use *are* when we are talking about more than one person or thing.
    *For example,   The girls **are** in the room.   The dogs **are** in the kennels.*

Write *is* or *are* in the spaces.

1. The sun _____ shining.

2. The girls _____ skipping.

3. The cars _____ racing.

4. The ladder _____ falling.

5. The ladders _____ falling.

6. The horses _____ galloping.

7. The stars _____ twinkling.

8. The horse _____ galloping.

9. The book _____ on the table.

10. The birds _____ in the nests.

We must be careful when we use *was* or *were*.

We use ***was*** when we are talking about one person or thing.
>   *For example,*   *The girl **was** on the swing.*
>   *The horse **was** in the stable.*

We use ***were*** when we are talking about more than one person or thing.
>   *For example,*   *The girls **were** on the swing.*
>   *The horses **were** in the stable.*

Write *was* or *were* in the spaces.

1. The stars _____ twinkling.

2. The cat _____ climbing the tree.

3. The chickens _____ pecking at the food.

4. The boat _____ sailing across the lake.

5. The bird _____ sitting on its nest.

6. The boys _____ in the garden.

7. The thief _____ in the room.

8. The cup _____ on the table.

9. Some toys _____ in the box.

10. Lots of butterflies _____ in the cage.

All words have different functions or uses. Some words tell us what people, animals and things are like. We call these words *adjectives*. Adjectives define nouns.

Example   a **tall** boy   an **angry** dog   a **sharp** knife

Which word best describes the noun?

1. The _____ **apple** was crunchy.
    (red   happy   silly)

2. The _____ **fire** warmed our toes.
    (cold   clean   hot)

3. A _____ **monster** chased them.
    (scary   little   pink)

4. The _____ **clothes** were put in the wash.
    (old   clean   muddy)

5. Five _____ **foals** ran around the paddock.
    (newborn   unhappy   soft)

6. The _____ **clouds** moved across the sky.
    (blue   grey   green)

7. The _____ old **car** was for sale.
    (battered   poor   new)

8. I think _____ **wool** is nice to touch.
    (dirty   cow's   soft)

9. The _____ **bully** teased the small boy.
    (handsome   cruel   tiny)

10. Jacob put on his new _____ **shoes**.
    (beach   school   elephant)

Adjectives **are words that describe or tell us more about people or things (nouns).**

For example,   a **smelly** fish   some **green** apples

1. In List A there are six adjectives. In List B there are six names. Can you write the adjective with the name it best describes? The first one has been done for you.

List A	List B		
windy	grass	**dirty**	**dishes**
broken	door	_____	_____
dirty	ball	_____	_____
rubber	window	_____	_____
open	weather	_____	_____
green	dishes	_____	_____

2. Select the adjective in the box that rhymes with the bold noun in the sentence. Write the adjective in the space.

white	tall	poor	pink
long	old	blue	deep

This is _____ **gold.**

This is a _____ **door.**

I have a_____ **kite.**

We swam in the _____ **creek.**

Sally is wearing a _____ **shoe.**

Our kitchen has a _____ **sink.**

She sang a _____ **song.**

We climbed over a _____ **wall.**

Prepositions are words that tell us where someone or something is.

Example

*The dog is **in** the kennel.*

*The cat is **under** the table.*

Look at the picture. Add the correct word in the space.

1. A squirrel is climbing _____ a tree.
   (up   down)

2. There are three eggs _____ the nest.
   (under   in)

3. The dog is hiding _____ the lounge chair.
   (over   under)

4. A kangaroo is hopping _____ a fence.
   (over   under)

5. The chair is _____ the television.
   (in   beside)

6. The girl is diving _____ the water.
   (into   up)

7. The clock is _____ the table.
   (above   on)

8. The cat is _____ the chairs.
   (above   between)

Conjunctions are words that join words or sentences together.

Example

John **and** Sue are at home.

We did not come **because** she was sick.

Choose the word that would best join the two parts of the sentence.

1. We will get wet _____ it begins to rain.

   (if   but)

2. I washed the dishes _____ dried them.

   (and   unless)

3. Bottles are made of glass _____ tables are made of wood.

   (when   but)

4. I was late for school _____ I slept in.

   (because   until)

5. I will not help _____ you try harder.

   (unless   that)

6. Lyndsey read a comic _____ she was waiting for her mother.

   (but   while)

7. The dog came _____ it heard me call.

   (when   unless)

8. We must leave here _____ it is ten o'clock.

   (and   before)

A sentence is a group of words that makes sense. A sentence always includes a verb, and often a noun.

Example

A dog can bark. — is a sentence because it tells us a complete thought.
A pony — is not a sentence because it does not tell us what the pony did.
bark a can dog — is not a sentence because it does not make sense.

Underline the sentence which matches each picture.

1.

The cat is feeding its kittens.
The farmer is feeding the hens.

2.

Sally is riding a bike.
Sally is playing a game.

3.

The boys are fishing in the river.
The boys are climbing trees.

4.

I am helping my mother iron the clothes.
I am helping my mother in the garden.

5.

Jack is eating an orange.
Jack is eating a hot dog.

6.

A kettle is on the table.
The eggs are in the nest.

7.

The cowboy is chasing the bull.
A dog is chasing a rabbit.

8.

The lady is cutting down a tree.
The lady is planting a tree.

Events in a story come in a certain order.

Read the stories, then put a (1) next to the part of the story that happened first, put (2) beside what happened next and so on.

A. One sunny day a farmer was feeding his hens. He filled a bucket with some corn. He opened the gate and went into the hen house. He threw the corn all over the ground. A small grey mouse came out of its hole and began to nibble the corn. The farmer threw the empty bucket at the mouse.

_____ A small grey mouse began to nibble the corn.

_____ The farmer threw the empty bucket at the mouse.

_____ The farmer filled a bucket with some corn.

_____ The farmer went into the hen house.

B. Yesterday Mrs Chan took Tran and Sally to the beach. The two children ran along the warm sand. They poked their toes into the water to see if it was warm. They ran and dived into the waves. Tran found some seaweed and threw it at Sally. Sally screamed because she thought it was a crab.

_____ They poked their toes into the water.

_____ Tran threw some seaweed at Sally.

_____ Sally screamed because she thought it was a crab.

_____ Mrs Chan took Tran and Sally to the beach.

Read the story, then circle the correct answer.

Muffy the puppy was happy, for today was a holiday and Peter would be able to take him to the park to play. Peter put on Muffy's red collar and tied a piece of rope to it for a lead.

When they got to the park Peter removed the rope and let Muffy run around. Muffy saw a black cat. He chased after it. The cat arched its back and scratched Muffy on the nose. The cat ran up the tree. Muffy yelped because his nose was sore. He ran to Peter. "That will teach you not to chase cats," said Peter.

1. Muffy was a kitten. / puppy.

2. Muffy's collar was blue. / red.

3. Peter tied a piece of rope / some cotton to Muffy's collar.

4. Peter took Muffy to the park / the school to play.

5. Muffy chased a yellow butterfly. / a black cat.

6. The cat scratched Muffy on his neck. / on his nose.

7. The black cat ran up a tree. / behind a tree.

8. Peter thought Muffy had learnt a lesson. / was a brave dog.

Read the story carefully, then answer the questions below.

Last night our large, black cat caught a small, grey bird.
My mother took the bird from the cat
and put it in her apron pocket.

Nouns

1. Which word is the name of an animal with four legs?

   _____

2. Which word is the name of a creature with feathers?

   _____

Adjectives

3. What word tells us the colour of the cat?

   _____

4. Which word tells us the size of the bird?

   _____

Pronouns

5. What word tells us who the cat belongs to?

   _____

6. What word also stands for mother?

   _____

7. What word also stands for the bird?

   _____

Verbs

8. What word tells us what the cat did?

   _____

The letters of the alphabet are:

a b c d e f g h i j k l m n o p q r s t u v w x y z

They can also be written this way. These are called capital letters.

A B C D E F G H I J K L M N O P Q R S T U V W X Y Z

A. *Draw lines to connect the letters that go together. One has been done for you.*

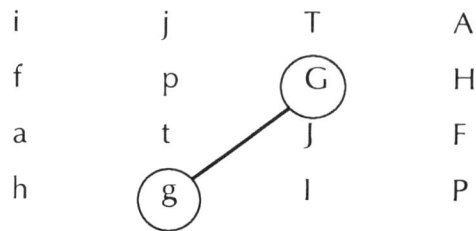

i	j	T	A
f	p	(G)	H
a	t	J	F
h	(g)	I	P

B. *Circle the letter that goes in the space.*

1. a b c _____ e f
    (r d z)

2. M N _____ P Q R
    (W A O)

3. G _____ I J K L
    (H B M)

4. p q r s t _____
    (u b f)

5. M N O _____ Q R
    (E P S)

6. l m n o p _____
    (e q x)

7. d e f g h _____
    (j i p)

8. S T U _____ W X
    (M V Z)

Sentences always begin with a capital letter and many end with a full stop.

Example

It is cold today.
The door is shut.

Circle the sentence in each pair that has the correct punctuation.
Write the other sentence correctly.

1. a dog is in the kennel.
   The birds are in the tree.

   _____

   _____

2. She helped me clean the room.
   i like eating ice-cream.

   _____

   _____

3. We played football yesterday
   She jumped over the fence.

   _____

   _____

4. Last night he came to my house.
   my friends are coming now.

   _____

   _____

5. It is nearly six o'clock.
   A bee is an insect

   _____

   _____

6. i like to read books.
   She is nine years old.

   _____

   _____

7. A box is on the table.
   some apples are in the bowl

   _____

   _____

8. my mother works at a garage
   Our father likes to tease us.

   _____

   _____

Sentences always begin with a capital letter and many end with a full stop.

Example   *I read a book.*
             She is in the room.

Add the capital letter and the full stop to each sentence.
Write the sentence underneath.

1. my dog is black

    _____

2. last week I won a race

    _____

3. the fireman lost his helmet

    _____

4. a cup is on the table

    _____

5. our teacher let us out early

    _____

6. his brother is ten years old

    _____

7. she rode her new bike to school

    _____

8. the book belongs to me

    _____

9. they planted a tree in the garden

    _____

10. parrots like to eat crackers.

    _____

Remember, sentences always begin with a capital letter and often end with a full stop.

For example,   She is baking some cakes.

We also use capital letters for the names of people, places, days, months, planets and so on.

For example,   Mr Jones, Joseph, Vietnam, Tuesday, April, Saturn

Add the capital letters and full stops where they are needed. Mark them in red.

1. my friend, julie, lives in sydney

2. last tuesday john went to england

3. mr jones is coming here next september

4. paul and sally live in wattle street

5. last night sam and julie came to our house

6. next april katy is buying paul a present

7. the two planets nearest the sun are mercury and venus

8. my friend, joseph jones, goes fishing every monday

9. the city of melbourne is in the state of victoria

10. my teacher, mrs jones, has a daughter named julie

A question always begins with a capital letter and ends with a question mark.

For example,   Where has she gone?

A statement always begins with a capital letter and ends with a full stop.

For example,   It is hot today.

Circle the sentence in each pair that has the correct punctuation.
Write the other sentence correctly.

1. Is he old enough to come?
    Where did Bill go.

    _____

    _____

2. It is starting to rain.
    The clock is on the wall?

    _____

    _____

3. why did he take the lollies?
    When are we going to leave?

    _____

    _____

4. A chair is beside the table.
    The lion is in the cage?

    _____

    _____

5. This book has lots of pages
    Four men are in the room.

    _____

    _____

6. My birthday is in March?
    Who is your best friend?

    _____

    _____

7. we went to the football.
    They played golf yesterday.

    _____

    _____

8. What is the name of your friend?
    why is he hiding under the table?

    _____

    _____

9. Have you read that book?
    My dog is barking loudly?

    _____

    _____

10. Where is my umbrella
    Why did you hit him?

    _____

    _____

PUNCTUATION — CAPITAL LETTERS, FULL STOPS AND QUESTION MARKS

Remember, all sentences begin with capital letters. Questions end with a question mark and statements end with a full stop.

For example,   *Where is he going?*
                It is hot today.

Remember, the names of people, places, months, days and so on all begin with capital letters.

For example,   *David, Mrs Smith, July, Monday, Melbourne*

Write each sentence correctly.

1. Where is peter going
    _____
    _____

2. is melbourne in victoria
    _____
    _____

3. he is leaving next monday
    _____
    _____

4. her birthday is in august
    _____
    _____

5. when is leanne's birthday
    _____
    _____

6. my teacher is mrs jones
    _____
    _____

7. why did callan steal the lollies from oona
    _____
    _____

8. what time does the next train to melbourne leave
    _____
    _____

9. is tom's birthday in september or october
    _____
    _____

10. is margaret going to the blue mountains
    _____
    _____

A question always begins with a capital letter and ends with a question mark.

Example

What is your name?
Is that our boat?

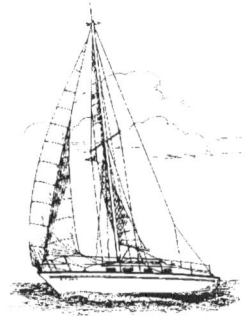

Look at each pair of sentences. Put a question mark at the end, if appropriate, and a full stop, if not. The first one has been done for you.

1. What is the time?
   He is coming now.

2. She is climbing up the tree
   Have you seen Terri

3. Where do the girls live
   That is my house over there

4. An insect has six legs
   How many legs has a spider

5. Did you see Paul yesterday
   Paul went to the football

6. I am going to Perth soon
   Where are you going at Easter

7. Jan likes to play netball
   Why didn't you get the ball

8. What is the name of that book
   My favourite hobby is reading

9. Is a wasp an insect
   Some spiders catch grasshoppers

10. He is not coming today
    When did he leave the room

Use a red pen to add the punctuation needed in the sentence below.
Write the sentence correctly.

Example

we saw bill last tuesday
We saw Bill last Tuesday.

Now do these.

1. sue and cathy are staying overnight

   _____

   _____

2. when did jack give ian the apple

   _____

   _____

3. last tuesday sam and paula went to melbourne

   _____

   _____

4. next christmas mike and con are going fishing in the yarra river

   _____

   _____

5. my friend paul smith goes to brisbane every december

   _____

   _____

6. i have lost my coat have you seen it

   _____

   _____

7. when are mike and nguyen going to vietnam with mrs smith

   _____

   _____

8. how far is it from sydney to melbourne i have been unable to find out

   _____

   _____

[ ] **denotes the unit to refer to.**

1. Use **a** or **an** in the spaces.
   I saw _____ egg on the table.
   Ned picked _____ flower.
   Freya is _____ happy girl.
   I ate _____ orange for lunch. **[1]**

2. Which word is the name of something?
   I saw an old giraffe at the zoo.
   (a) old   (b) giraffe   (c) saw   **[2,3,4]**

3. Choose the correct word to fill the space.
   There is a _____ of bees.
   (a) flock   (b) bunch   (c) swarm   **[5]**

4. Which two of these words should begin with a capital letter?

mouse	tomato	july
peter	cup	book	**[6,7]**

5. Make each of these mean more than one:

one dog:	two _____	**[8]**
one glass:	three _____	**[9]**
one fly	five _____	**[10]**

6. Which word tells us what Sam did?
   Last night Sam climbed over the fence in the backyard.
   (a) night   (b) over   (c) climbed   **[11,12]**

7. Use **is** or **are** in the spaces.
   The stars _____ shining.
   The dog _____ old.   **[13]**

8. Use **was** or **were** in the spaces.
   The girl _____ here before.
   The boys _____ coming.   **[14]**

9. Which word describes the car?
   The blue car roared down the freeway.
   (a) roared   (b) down   (c) blue   **[15, 16]**

10. Which word tells us the place Jack is?
    Jack tripped and fell down the hill.
    (a) down   (b) tripped   (c) fell   **[17]**

11. Use one of the words to join the sentences.
    I could not come _____ I was ill.
    (a) until   (b) because   (c) soon   **[18]**

12. Which of these is a sentence?
    (a) up in the tree
    (b) I saw John.
    (c) dog man bit a the   **[19, 20, 21, 22]**

Punctuate each sentence correctly.

13. he is in the kitchen   **[23, 24, 25]**

    _____

14. my two friends are sally and susan

    _____

    _____

    [24, 25, 26]

15. when will paul arrive in melbourne

    _____

    _____

    [27, 28,29]

GRAMMAR

UNIT 1 Using A or AN
1. **an** apple **a** banana 2. **an** egg **an** axe
3. **a** dog **a** kitten 4. **an** arm **a** leg
5. **an** oar **a** sail 6. **an** insect **a** bird
7. **an** oven **a** heater 8. **an** ostrich **an** elephant
9. **an** even **an** odd 10. **a** young dog, **an** old dog

UNIT 2 Nouns
1. dog 2. car 3. bike 4. key
5. cat 6. cake 7. rabbit 8. bones
9. **Mum**, **Dad**, **Ned** and **Freya** were going to the **zoo**. They caught the **bus** into **town**, the **ferry** across the **harbour** and the **cablecar** to the **entrance** of the **zoo**. "I want to see the **monkeys**," cried **Freya**. "I want to look at the **tigers**," shouted Ned. "I want to sit down and have a **rest**," said **Mum**, even though it wasn't even **lunchtime** yet. "Not yet," said **Dad**. "We'll let our little **animals** see some of the **zoo**'s big **animals** first, then we'll sit under that **tree** and have some **food**."

UNIT 3 Nouns
1. star 2. egg 3. bee 4. shoe
5. cow 6. frog 7. car 8. fire

UNIT 4 Nouns
1. magpie emu eagle
2. apple apricot plum
3. desk chair table
4. rose daffodil violet
5. milk soda cola
6. cake tart meat
7. fly moth butterfly
8. shoe sandal slippers
9. tie shirt dress
10. kite plane airship

UNIT 5 Collective Nouns
1. flock 2. swarm 3. team 4. bunch
5. herd 6. fleet 7. litter 8. forest
9. bundle 10. packet

UNIT 6 Proper Nouns
1. Monday 2. Susan 3. April 4. Friday
5. Melbourne 6. Katy 7. September
8. England 9-12. Self-correcting

UNIT 7 Proper Nouns
People in boxes: Joshua, Gina, Grandad, Wendy, Mrs Smith, Michelle, Mr Jones
Months and days are: Tuesday, Friday, July, August, Sunday, June, December
Places are: Albania, Lithgow, Africa, Paris, Fiji, Newcastle

1. Saturday, Sunday 2. Monday
3. Friday 4. Wednesday 5. Monday
6. Tuesday 7. Self-correcting

UNIT 8 Singular and Plural
Plurals in boxes: windows pages chairs
birds trees roads
1. cows 2. eggs 3. beds 4. toys
5. rats 6. shops 7. stars 8. pigs
9. balls 10. bears

UNIT 9 Singular and Plural
1. bushes 2. peaches 3. foxes 4. buses
5. boxes 6. glasses 7. brushes 8. churches
9. classes 10. matches

UNIT 10 Singular and Plural
donkeys, toys ponies, babies
spray, sprays tray, trays day, days key, keys
toy, toys boy, boys buoy, buoys pray, prays

two **feet** lots of **teeth**
three **men** two **children**

UNIT 11 Verbs
1. sitting 2. driving 3. jumping 4. eating
5. kicking 6. reading 7. pushing 8. writing
9. climbing 10. riding

UNIT 12 Verbs
1. draw 2. dig 3. catch 4. fry
5. write 6. bend 7. fly 8. eat
9. play 10. help

UNIT 13 IS and ARE
1. is 2. are 3. are 4. is
5. are 6. are 7. are 8. is
9. is 10. are

UNIT 14 WAS and WERE
1. were 2. was 3. were 4. was
5. was 6. were 7. was 8. was
9. were 10. were

UNIT 15 Adjectives
1. red 2. hot 3. scary 4. muddy
5. newborn 6. grey 7. battered 8. soft
9. cruel 10. school

UNIT 16 Adjectives
dirty dishes windy weather broken window
rubber ball open door green grass
old gold blue shoe poor door
pink sink white kite long song
deep creek tall wall

UNIT 17   Prepositions
1. up   2. in   3. under   4. over
5. beside   6. into   7. on   8. between

UNIT 18   Conjunctions
1. if   2. and   3. but   4. because
5. unless   6. while   7. when   8. before

UNIT 19   Sentences
1. The farmer is feeding the hens. 2. Sally is riding a bike. 3. The boys are fishing in the river.   4. Helping my mother in the garden.   5.   Jack is eating a hot dog.
6. The eggs are in the nest. 7. The cowboy is chasing the bull.   8. The lady is planting a tree.

UNIT 20   Sequencing
A. 3, 4, 1, 2 B. 2, 3, 4, 1

UNIT 21   Comprehension
1. puppy   2. red   3. a piece of rope
4. the park 5. a black cat 6. on his nose
7. up a tree 8. had learnt a lesson

UNIT 22   Grammar Test Check
1. cat   2. bird   3. black   4. small
5. our   6. her   7. it   8. caught

PUNCTUATION
UNIT 23   Capital Letters
A. Self-correcting
B.   1. d   2. O
3. H   4. u   5. P
6. q   7. i   8. V

UNIT 24   Capitals and Full Stops
1. The birds are in the tree.
2. She helped me clean the room.
3. She jumped over the fence.
4. Last night he came to my house.
5. It is nearly six o'clock.
6. She is nine years old.
7. A box is on the table.
8. Our father likes to tease us.

UNIT 25   Capitals and Full Stops
1. My dog is black.
2. Last week I won a race.
3. The fireman lost his helmet.
4. A cup is on the table.
5. Our teacher let us out early.
6. His brother is ten years old.
7. She rode her new bike to school.
8. The book belongs to me.
9. They planted a tree in the garden.
10. Parrots like to eat crackers.

UNIT 26   Capital Letters
1. My friend, Julie, lives in Sydney.
2. Last Tuesday John went to England.
3. Mr Jones is coming here next September.
4. Paula and Sally live in Wattle Street.
5. Last night Sam and Julie came to our house.
6. Next April Katy is buying Paul a present.
7. The two planets nearest the Sun are Mercury and Venus.
8. My friend, Joseph Jones, goes fishing every Monday.
9. The city of Melbourne is in the state of Victoria.
10. My teacher, Mrs Jones, has a daughter named Julie.

UNIT 27   Statements and Questions
1. Is he old enough to come? 2. It is starting to rain.
3. When are we going to leave? 4. A chair is beside the table.   5. Four men are in the room.   6. Who is your best friend? 7. They played golf yesterday.
8. What is the name of your friend?   9. Have you read that book?   10. Why did you hit him?

UNIT 28   Punctuation
1. Where is Peter going?   2. Is Melbourne in Victoria?   3. He is leaving next Monday.
4. Her birthday is in August.   5. When is Leanne's birthday?   6. My teacher is Mrs Jones.
7. Why did Callan steal the lollies from Oona?
8. What time does the next train to Melbourne leave?
9. Is Tom's birthday in September or October?
10. Is Margaret going to the Blue Mountains?

UNIT 29   Questions
1. ? .   2. . ?   3. ? .   4. . ?
5. ? .   6. . ?   7. . ?   8. ? .
9. ? .   10. . ?

UNIT 30   Punctuation Test Check
1. Sue and Cathy are staying overnight.
2. When did Jack give Ian the apple?
3. Last Tuesday Sam and Paula went to Melbourne.
4. Next Christmas Mike and Con are going fishing in the Yarra River.
5. My friend, Paul Smith, goes to Brisbane every December.
6. I have lost my coat. Have you seen it?
7. When are Mike and Nguyen going to Vietnam with Mrs Smith?
8. How far is it from Sydney to Melbourne? I have been unable to find out.

MASTERY TEST ANSWERS YEAR 3
1. an, a, a, an   2. giraffe   3. swarm
4. July, Peter   5. two dogs, three glasses, five flies
6. climbed   7. are, is   8. was, were
9. blue   10. down   11. because
12. I saw John.   13. He is in the kitchen.
14. My two friends are Sally and Susan.
15. When will Paul arrive in Melbourne?

GRAMMAR

UNIT 1   **Nouns**
1. stable   2. hospital   3. silo   4. kitchen
5. hangar   6. dentist   7. chemist   8. pilot
9. clown   10. casher

UNIT 2   **Collective Nouns**
1. herd   2. bunch   3. litter   4. swarm
5. batch   6. string   7. crowd   8. pack
9. suit   10. set

UNIT 3   **Proper Nouns**
1. Monday   2. July   3. Julie   4. Michael
5. Melbourne   6. September   7. England   8. Venus
9. August   10. Helen

UNIT 4   **Singular and Plural**
1. tables   2. buses   3. dresses   4. bushes
5. matches   6. wishes   7. foxes   8. dishes
9. boxes   10. apples   11. glasses   12. stitches

UNIT 5   **Singular and Plural**
1. toys   2. berries   3. cherries   4. keys
5. cities   6. flies   7. donkeys   8. ladies
9. stories   10. turkeys

UNIT 6   **Singular and Plural**
1. halves   2. thieves   3. scarves   4. knives
5. loaves   6. wolves   7. teeth   8. men
9. mice   10. children   11. geese   12. women

UNIT 7   **Verbs**
1. peeling   2. ringing   3. falling   4. boiling
5. ticking   6. threw   7. grew   8. rowed
9. cried   10. played

UNIT 8   **Verbs**
1. croaking   2. blowing   3. falling   4. cutting
5. winning   6. stopping   7. swimming   8. saving
9. hiding   10. shining   11. taking   12. moving

UNIT 9   **Verbs – Tense**
1. rowed   2. played   3. kicked   4. refused
5. wasted   6. decided   7. swam   8. spoke
9. sank   10. patted   11. mopped   12. stopped

UNIT 10   **Agreement of Subject and Verb**
1. like   2. does   3. comes   4. put
5. goes   6. come   7. plays   8. write
9. reads   10. runs

UNIT 11   **Agreement of Subject and Verb**
1. were   2. is   3. have   4. are
5. was   6. are   7. were   8. has
9. has   10. was   11. were   12. are

UNIT 12   **Pronouns**
1. he, they   2. her, they   3. we, him   4. she, her
5. me, mine   6. him, his   7. us, ours   8. them, theirs

UNIT 13   **Prepositions**
1. into   2. up   3. over   4. under
5. in   6. above   7. between   8. against

UNIT 14   **Adverbs**
1. quickly   2. greedily   3. now   4. neatly
5. gently   6. angrily   7. loudly   8. brightly
9. sleepily   10. proudly

UNIT 15   **Adjectives**
1. woollen   2. yellow   3. deep   4. comfortable
5. six   6. large   7. dirty   8. rich
9. blue   10. open   11. stale   12. rusty

UNIT 16   **Conjunctions**
1. if   2. until   3. although   4. because
5. and   6. before   7. until   8. and
9. when   10. but

UNIT 17   **Sentences**
1. 30   2. November   3. July   4. 29
5. 31   6. September   7. October   8. 31

UNIT 18   **Sentences**
1. b   2. a   3. a   4. a
5. b   6. a   7. b   8. a

UNIT 19   **Sentences**
1. b   2. a   3. b   4. b
5. a   6. a   7. a   8. a

UNIT 20   **Grammar Test Check**
1. dog   2. Joanne   3. barked   4. climbed
5. black   6. tall   7. loudly   8. over
9. she   10. as

PUNCTUATION

UNIT 21   **Capital Letters and Full Stops**
1. The cat is in the cot.   2. It is nearly lunchtime.
3. John is my best friend.   4. My mother works at the supermarket.   5. She is nine years old.   6. A spider has eight legs.   7. She helped me clean the room.
8. She saw him at the disco.

UNIT 22   **Capital Letters**
1. My best friend is Cathy.   2. Michael is going to England next year.   3. Tom and Mary live in Sydney.
4. Chan and Ken both come from Vietnam.
5. When Sam was in Melbourne he met Jack in Bourke Street.
6. Mrs Smith and Mr Jones returned from Canada last week.
7. Tom told us that the city of Venice was in Italy.
8. John, Peter and Effy, who all live in Perth, Western Australia, are doing a project on Asia.

UNIT 23   Capital Letters

1. Last Monday my friend, Brian, came to my home.
2. Next April Paul and I are going to Vietnam.
3. George was fishing in the Yarra River when he saw Sue.
4. The last Tuesday in December is Christmas Day.
5. Maggie and Martin both live in Wattle Street in Melbourne.
6. Andrew and Darcy caught the train in Spencer Street.
7. I was told by Alfie last Wednesday that the closest planet to the Sun is Mercury.
8. It is nearly Easter and next week it will be Good Friday.

UNIT 24   Questions

1. ? .   2. . ?   3. . ?   4. ? .
5. ? .   6. ? .   7. . ?   8. ? .

UNIT 25   Punctuation

1. What is the time? It is nearly ten o'clock.
2. She will play netball. What sport is Mary playing today?
3. Why is the baby crying? It is crying because it is hungry.
4. Is it time for us to go? We will have to wait five more minutes.
5. Who owns that bicycle? The bicycle belongs to me.
6. When is the bus due? It should arrive soon.
7. How did Jack get the ball down? He cut off a branch of the tree.
8. In which month is Christmas? It is in December.
9. I bought it at the canteen. Where did you get that pie?
10. It is our turn to empty the bins. Whose job is it to do the bins today?

UNIT 26   Questions and Statements

1. I met the new boy. Have you met him?
2. I don't like pizza. Do you like it?
3. What colour is a penguin? It is black and white.
4. Billy is crying loudly. Do you know why?
5. How many legs has a spider? It has eight legs.
6. This is Rob's new bicycle. When did he get it?
7. My puppy is still missing. Have you seen it?
8. We are one short for the team. Has Phil arrived yet?
9. I can't lift this chair. Will you help me?
10. Do you remember where I put my glasses? I had them only ten minutes ago.

UNIT 27   Punctuation

1. Michael has a new puppy. Have you seen it?
2. I have lots to do. Will you help me?3. Ian doesn't like David. Do you like him?
4. I found this pencil. Does it belong to you?
5. I liked that movie. Did you see it?
6. What colour is a magpie? It is black and white.
7. How many legs has a beetle? It has six legs.

8. What is your favourite food? It is pizza.
9. When is Mary's birthday? It is in April.
10. When is Christmas Day? It is in December.

UNIT 28   The Comma

1. The three colours of the Australian flag are red, white and blue.
2. The planets closest to the Sun are Mercury, Venus, Earth and Mars.
3. My favourite foods are apples, bananas, pizzas and chocolate.
4. Flies, bees, beetles, ants and grasshoppers are all insects.
5. Carly, Jack, Paul, Martin and Annie are the oldest children in our grade.
6. Four types of vegetables are potatoes, tomatoes, lettuces and peas.
7. The dog ran along the fence, across the road, down the steps, into the yard and through the front door.
8. I helped him sweep the path, wash the dishes, hang out the clothes, clean the fireplace and cut the lawn.

UNIT 29   The Apostrophe

1. isn't   2. can't   3. It's   4. We're
5. who's   6. wasn't   7. didn't   8. won't
9. you'll   10. We've

UNIT 30   Punctuation Test Check

1. My best friends are Joe and Robyn.
2. When are you going to England?
3. Last Tuesday Mr Smith took Sharon to Perth.
4. Is John's birthday in April or June?
5. Last Thursday Sam went fishing in the Murray River with Jock and Toni.
6. Con has lost his new pencil case. Have you seen it?
7. Josh planted carrots, peas, beans, potatoes and tomatoes in the garden.
8. Daniel looked under the table, on top of the chair, near the television, and in the bedroom but could not find his knife.

MASTERY TEST ANSWERS YEAR 4

1. tree   2. school   3. September, Paul
4. seven dishes   5. two cities
6. three knives   7. climbed   8. taking
9. stopped   10. like   11. were
12. he   13. into   14. yesterday
15. large   16. when
17. The girls played in the rain.
18. My friend Mel went to Melbourne last Thursday.
19. Where did John go?
20. I ate pies, chips, apples, pears and lollies for lunch.
21. I must not be late for school.

Nouns are naming words. They are used to name a person, place, thing or feeling.

For example, dog, cat, stone, step, ice-cream

Example   Circle the correct noun that answers the question.
Which noun is a spider's home?

(a) *house*   (b) *web*   (c) *kennel*

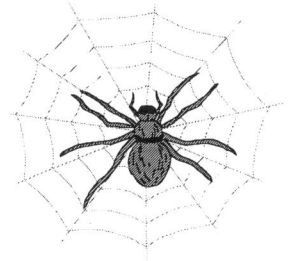

Now do each of these.

1. Which noun is the home of a horse?
   (a) sty   (b) stable   (c) hive

2. Which noun is a place where sick people stay?
   (a) igloo   (b) pen   (c) hospital

3. Which noun is a place to store grain?
   (a) garage   (b) office   (c) silo

4. Which noun is a place you can cook in?
   (a) kitchen   (b) bathroom   (c) zoo

5. Which noun is a place where aeroplanes are kept?
   (a) burrow   (b) supermarket   (c) hangar

6. Which noun is a person who cares for our teeth?
   (a) clown   (b) dentist   (c) teacher

7. Which noun is a person who sells medicines?
   (a) greengrocer   (b) umpire   (c) chemist

8. Which noun is a person who flies an aeroplane?
   (a) pilot   (b) carpenter   (c) nurse

9. Which noun is a person who makes us laugh at a circus?
   (a) florist   (b) clown   (c) farmer

10. Which noun is a person who checks out our groceries in a supermarket?
    (a) cashier   (b) baker   (c) doctor

Some nouns are the names of collections of people, animals or things. These are called collective nouns.

For example, a **flock** *of sheep*

Example Choose the correct collective noun to fill the space.

I saw a _____ *of birds.*

(a) bunch   (b) flock   (c) herd

Now choose the best collective noun to fill the spaces.

1. We saw a _____ of cattle.
   (a) flock   (b) batch   (c) herd

2. Joanne has a _____ of purple grapes.
   (a) bunch   (b) pack   (c) forest

3. Ray's dog has a _____ of puppies.
   (a) crowd   (b) pack   (c) litter

4. A _____ of insects bit me.
   (a) swarm   (b) pack   (c) herd

5. The baker heated the _____ of loaves.
   (a) swarm   (b) batch   (c) bunch

6. She wore a _____ of pearls around her neck.
   (a) bunch   (b) pack   (c) string

7. There was a big _____ of people at the football.
   (a) swarm   (b) crowd   (c) herd

8. He had a _____ of cards in his pocket.
   (a) pack   (b) forest   (c) flock

9. My dad has a new _____ of clothes.
   (a) school   (b) suit   (c) litter

10. There is a _____ of tools in the shed.
    (a) set   (b) swarm   (c) clock

Some nouns are the names of people, places and things.
These are called proper nouns.
Proper nouns always begin with a capital letter.

For example, Julie, Monday, July, Mrs Jones

My name is Julie.

Choose the word that is a proper noun.
Write it with a capital letter.
The first one has been done for you.

1. water   monday   letter
    **Monday**

6. september   school   pencil
    _____

2. july   paper   house
    _____

7. lolly   chair   england
    _____

3. sister   julie   street
    _____

8. bird   venus   clock
    _____

4. michael   uncle   fork
    _____

9. bush   august   road
    _____

5. melbourne   grass   bottle
    _____

10. helen   book   butter
    _____

Nouns can be singular (*one*) or plural (*more than one*). Most nouns make their plural by adding -s.

For example, one **cow** — two **cows**,   one **bike** — five **bikes**
                one **town** — two **towns**

However, words that end in **-s, -sh, -ch** or **-x**
add **-es** to make their plurals.

For example,   **gas** — **gases**   **bush** — **bushes**

Make the word in brackets mean more than one. Write it in the space in the sentence.

1. There are two _____ in the room. (table)

2. I saw three _____ in the carpark. (bus)

3. Cath put all her _____ on the bed. (dress)

4. There are lots of _____ growing in the garden. (bush)

5. There are five _____ left in the box. (match)

6. The good fairy gave her three _____. (wish)

7. We saw two _____ on their lairs. (fox)

8. I have dried all the _____. (dish)

9. I put the toys in the two _____. (box)

10. I ate two _____ for lunch. (apple)

11. There are three _____ on the table. (glass)

12. The doctor sewed up the cut with seven _____. (stitch)

Nouns that end in -y and have a vowel before the -y simply add -s to make the plural. The vowels are a, e, i, o, u.

For example, one **boy** *— two* **boys**   *one* **day** *— three* **days**

For nouns that end in **-y** but have a consonant before the **-y**, change the **-y** into **-i** and add **-es** to make the plural.

For example, one **city** *— two* **cities**   *one* **dairy** *— three* **dairies**

Choose the correct plural of the word to fill the space.

1. I have lots of _____.
   (toies, toys)

2. There were lots of _____ on the vine.
   (berrys, berries)

3. I ate four _____ for lunch.
   (cherries, cherrys)

4. I put all the _____ in the cupboard.
   (keys, keies)

5. There are some big _____ in Australia.
   (cities, citys)

6. I caught six _____ in the net.
   (flys, flies)

7. There are four _____ in the paddock.
   (donkeys, donkeies)

8. Some _____ were in the room.
   (ladys, ladies)

9. Our teacher read us four _____ at lunchtime.
   (storys, stories)

10. On our farm we have over fifty _____.
    (turkeies, turkeys)

Some nouns that end in -f make their plural by changing the -f to -v and adding -es.
For example, **loaf — loaves**   **leaf — leaves**

However, there are some exceptions.
For example, **chief — chiefs**   **roof — roofs**

Some nouns make their plurals by changing vowels
(for example, **one foot — two feet**) or by adding **-en,**
for example, **child — children**

Make the word in brackets mean more than one. Write it in the space.

1. I cut the cakes into _____.
    (half)

2. The two _____ were
    caught by the police. (thief)

3. There are some nice
    _____ in that shop.
    (scarf)

4. There are six _____ on
    the table. (knife)

5. The baker showed me the four
    _____ of bread. (loaf)

6. The two _____ tried to
    catch the young deer. (wolf)

7. The dentist pulled out two of his
    _____. (tooth)

8. There were three _____
    in the cafe. (man)

9. I saw three _____ in the
    shed. (mouse)

10. There are over twenty
    _____ in our year. (child)

11. We cooked two _____ for
    Christmas Day. (goose)

12. I saw seven _____ at the
    disco. (woman)

Verbs are words that tell us what people are doing or have done. They are *doing words*.

Example

Jim is **pushing** the pram.

Emmy is **climbing** a tree.

Choose the best verb to complete each sentence.

1. Paul is _____ an orange.
   (a) crying   (b) peeling   (c) ringing

2. Margot is _____ the bell.
   (a) singing   (b) playing   (c) ringing

3. The rain is _____ from the sky.
   (a) falling   (b) laughing   (c) skipping

4. The water in the kettle is _____.
   (a) thinking   (b) sitting   (c) boiling

5. The clock is _____.
   (a) sailing   (b) ticking   (c) beating

6. The girl _____ the ball to me.
   (a) threw   (b) played   (c) jumped

7. A tree _____ in the backyard.
   (a) flew   (b) grew   (c) looked

8. The children _____ the boat across the lake.
   (a) rowed   (b) painted   (c) flowed

9. The baby _____ when it was hungry.
   (a) cried   (b) grew   (c) moved

10. The children _____ games in the yard.
    (a) acted   (b) played   (c) cried

To tell us someone or something is doing something right now, we add *-ing*.

For example,   *The tree* **grows**   *The tree is* **growing**

Sometimes we have to make changes to the verb. For example, we may have to double the last letter.
For example,   *the boy* **steps**.   *The boy is* **stepping**

If the word ends in a silent *-e* we must drop the *-e* to add *-ing*.
For example,   *I* **hide.**   *I am* **hiding**.

Make the verb in brackets end in -ing. Write the word in the space.

1. I can hear a frog _____.
   (croak)

2. The leaves are _____
   across the lawn. (blow)

3. The old house is _____
   down. (fall)

4. Tommy is _____ the
   string. (cut)

5. Our team is _____ the
   game. (win)

6. The cars are _____ at the
   corner. (stop)

7. Will is _____ across the
   pool. (swim)

8. Ian is _____ all his money.
   (save)

9. The snake is _____ under
   the rock. (hide)

10. The stars are _____
    brightly. (shine)

11. The thief is _____ the
    watches. (take)

12. We are _____ to another
    house next week. (move)

Look at these two sentences.

> The girls **know** their work. (present tense — now, at the present time.)
> The girls **knew** their work. (past tense — in the past.)

To make their past tense, some verbs:
(a) simply add **-ed**, for example, **defeated**.
(b) drop the **-e** and add **-ed** if the verb ends in **-e**, for example, **decide — decided**.
(c) change a letter, for example, **ring** (present) — **rang** (past).
(d) double the last letter before adding **-ed**, for example, **plan — planned**.

Write the past tense of the verb in the space.

1. Matt _____ the boat across the lake yesterday. (row)

2. Last night I _____ Scrabble with my parents. (play)

3. This morning Tommy _____ Jack on the leg. (kick)

4. Kim _____ to help me yesterday. (refuse)

5. Last week Dave _____ a lot of money buying lollies. (waste)

6. Yesterday I _____ I would help my parents. (decide)

7. Yesterday Nick _____ across the lake. (swim)

8. Last Tuesday, the principal _____ to our class. (speak)

9. When we threw them in the water, the stones _____ quickly. (sink)

10. This morning I _____ Cal's new dog. (pat)

11. Helen _____ the floor last night. (mop)

12. The policeman _____ the car at ten o'clock this morning. (stop)

The subject of a sentence must always agree with its verb. If the subject is singular, then the verb must be singular. If the subject is plural, then the verb must be plural.

For example,   *The boy* _____ *to bed early. (go, goes)*
The subject is **boy**, which is singular, so we must use the singular verb **goes**.

For example,   *The boys* _____ *to bed early. (go, goes)*
The subject is **boys**, which is plural, so we must use the plural verb **go**.

Choose the correct verb and write it in the space.

1. All dogs _____ bones.
   (like   likes)

2. My sister _____ her work neatly.
   (do   does)

3. Tim _____ to school early every day.
   (come   comes)

4. The children always _____ their books away neatly.
   (put   puts)

5. He _____ to a football match every Saturday.
   (go   goes)

6. The teachers _____ to our supermarket often.
   (come   comes)

7. John _____ a violin in the school band.
   (play   plays)

8. The children on camp _____ to their parents every day.
   (write   writes)

9. My teacher _____ us a story every Monday.
   (read   reads)

10. Michelle often gets into trouble because she _____ across the lawn.
    (run   runs)

The subject of a sentence must always agree with its verb.

If the subject is singular, it must have a singular verb.
For example, **(is, was, has)** *always go with* **singular** *subjects.*
          The boy **is** *angry.*   *The girl* **was** *here.*   *The girl* **has** *black hair.*

If the subject is plural, it must have a plural verb.
For example,   *The boys* **are** *angry.*   *The girls* **were** *here.*   *The girls* **have** *black hair.*

Choose the correct word to fill the space.

1. The boys _____ late for school.
   (was   were)

2. The star _____ shining brightly.
   (is   are)

3. Our guests _____ arrived.
   (has   have)

4. Paul and Joanne _____ in the room.
   (is   are)

5. David _____ playing when the bomb exploded.
   (was   were)

6. Oranges and apples _____ my two favourite fruits.
   (is   are)

7. They _____ frightened by the savage dog.
   (was   were)

8. Tommy _____ got the best mark for spelling.
   (has   have)

9. Perhaps she _____ heard the news by now.
   (has   have)

10. It _____ very warm at school yesterday.
    (was   were)

11. The oranges _____ wrapped in silver paper.
    (was   were)

12. We _____ leaving before ten o'clock.
    (is   are)

Pronouns are words we use instead of a noun. Look at these sentences.

John hit at the ball but John missed the ball.

Instead of repeating **John** and **ball**, we could write:
*John hit at the ball but **he** missed **it.***

Here are some pronouns we often use:

I	we	me	us	it
you		you		
he/she/it	they	him/her	them	

Choose the pronoun to go in each space.

1. One day Simon's father came home
   from work.
   _____ had some coins in his pocket.
   _____ were very shiny.
   (they, he)

2. Fraser's mother said she was going to the
   supermarket for milk.
   Fraser went with _____ and _____
   bought several cartons.
   (her, they)

3. I am going to the disco with my friend.
   _____ will meet at 7.30.
   I will wait for _____ at my house.
   (we, him)

4. Fran's sister made a cake.
   _____ mixed some flour and water.
   Fran helped _____ add the eggs.
   (her, she)

5. The book belongs to _____.
   The book is _____.
   (me, mine)

6. The birds belong to _____.
   The birds are _____.
   (his, him)

7. The keys belong to _____.
   The keys are _____.
   (ours, us)

8. The balls belong to _____.
   The balls are _____.
   (them, theirs)

Prepositions are words that tell us the place or position of a person or thing.

Example   The dog is **in** the kennel.
The cat is **under** the table.

Look closely at the pictures, then the accompanying sentences.
Use one of the prepositions in the box to fill the space in each sentence.

between	under	over	into
against	in	up	above

1.
He is shooting the ball _____ the hoop.

2.
A spider is climbing _____ the tree.

3.
The athlete is jumping _____ the hurdle.

4.
The textbooks are _____ the apple.

5.
A boy is fishing _____ the creek.

6.
The sun is _____ the mountains.

7.
The teacher is standing _____ the students.

8.
The dog is leaning _____ his owner.

Adverbs tell *how, when, where* or *why* something happened.

Example

The men walked **slowly.**
The pony is standing over **there.**

Fill each space with the most appropriate adverb.

1. The frightened boy ran _____
   inside.
   (slowly, quickly, sweetly)

2. The hungry girls ate the cake
   _____.
   (greedily, loudly, brightly)

3. We must leave right _____.
   (soon, now, tomorrow)

4. Chris wrote _____ in his book.
   (roughly, neatly, greedily)

5. The mother spoke _____ to
   the little baby.
   (easily, gently, neatly)

6. The teacher growled _____.
   (slowly, happily, angrily)

7. The baby cried _____.
   (loudly, happily, correctly)

8. The sun was shining _____.
   (brightly, slowly, quietly)

9. The tired girl nodded her head
   _____.
   (sleepily, angrily, kindly)

10. She accepted the prize _____.
    (sadly, proudly, loudly)

Adjectives are words that tell us more about nouns.

Example The sentence "I saw a dog" does not tell us much about the dog but if we say "I saw a **big**, **black** dog", we now have more information.

Choose the best adjective to fill the space in each sentence.

1. Rebecca wore a _____ jumper to school.
   (fat, tall, woollen)

2. A ripe banana is usually _____.
   (green, blue, yellow)

3. This is a very _____ river.
   (happy, deep, ripe)

4. I am sitting in a _____ chair.
   (comfortable, sunny, loyal)

5. An insect has _____ legs.
   (five, eight, six)

6. An elephant is _____ but an ant is tiny.
   (purple, large, pretty)

7. These muddy shirts are very _____.
   (clean, dirty, blue)

8. A person with a lot of money is _____.
   (poor, old, rich)

9. The Australian flag is red, white and _____.
   (grey, yellow, blue)

10. I shut the _____ door.
    (open, rich, deep)

11. This old bread is _____.
    (stale, merry, wise)

12. The old knife has become quite _____.
    (cold, rusty, cheeky)

Conjunctions are words that join together other words or groups of words.

Example

Jack **and** Jill went home.
She did not come **because** she was ill.

Choose the conjunction that would best join the sentences.

1. The grass will die _____ it
    does not rain soon.
    (if   when)

2. We must wait here _____ the
    rain stops.
    (because   until)

3. Maisie did not help me _____
    she said she would.
    (although   until)

4. I ran quickly _____ I didn't
    want to miss the school bus.
    (unless   because)

5. James read a comic _____ I
    played a game.
    (and   whether)

6. We must leave _____ it is
    seven o'clock.
    (before   unless)

7. Let us sit here _____ the sun
    sets.
    (until   because)

8. I saw a dog _____ a cat on the
    lawn.
    (while   and)

9. We must leave _____ it begins
    to get dark.
    (when   whether)

10. The dog tried to catch the rabbit
    _____ the rabbit was too fast.
    (but   and)

Read the following carefully, then answer the questions below.

Thirty days hath September,
April, June and November,
All the rest have thirty-one,
Excepting February alone,
Which has twenty-eight days clear,
And twenty-nine in each leap year.

	SEPTEMBER					
S	M	T	W	T	F	S
	1	2	3	4	5	6
7	8	9	10	11	12	13
14	15	16	17	18	19	20
21	22	33	24	25	26	27
29	30					

Circle the correct answer.

1. How many days are there in June?

    (a) 28   (b) 30   (c) 31

2. Which of these months has thirty days?

    (a) August (b) November (c) January

3. Which of these months has thirty-one days?

    (a) July (b) February (c) April

4. How many days were there in February in a leap year?

    (a) 29   (b) 28   (c) 31

5. How many days are there in December?

    (a) 29   (b) 31   (c) 30

6. Which of these months has only thirty days?

    (a) March   (b) September   (c) July

7. Which of these months has the most days?

    (a) April (b) October (c) February

8. How many days are there in May?

    (a) 31   (b) 30   (c) 29

It is important you understand the information that is provided for you when you read a sentence. This will help you make correct conclusions from the things you read.

Read the question, then circle what you think is the most suitable answer.

1. Why do children like lollies?
   (a) They like them because they are bitter.
   (b) They like them because they are sweet.

2. Why do children go to school?
   (a) Children go to school to learn to read and write.
   (b) Children go to school because they like eating ice-cream.

3. Why do babies cry?
   (a) They cry because they are hungry.
   (b) They cry because they can't drive motor cars.

4. Why is Alana laughing?
   (a) She is laughing because she is happy.
   (b) She is laughing because she is sad.

5. Why do we wear hats on hot days?
   (a) We wear them to keep our heads warm.
   (b) We wear them so the sun won't burn our skin.

6. Why is Tan putting on his boots?
   (a) He is putting on his boots because he is going to play football.
   (b) He is putting on his boots because he is going to bed.

7. Why do cows wear bells?
   (a) Cows wear bells because their horns don't work.
   (b) Cows wear bells so the farmer knows where they are.

8. Why do birds build nests?
   (a) They build nests to lay their eggs in.
   (b) They build nests so their friends can stay with them.

It is important that when we read a story we understand fully what we have read.

Did you know all birds lay eggs? Some birds build a nest in which to lay their eggs. The mother bird sits on the eggs to keep them warm. The baby bird grows inside the egg. The yellow yolk makes food for the growing baby bird. After a time, the baby bird pecks on the inside of the shell. The shell breaks and the baby hatches.

The baby bird's parents feed it until it is able to fly and leave the nest.

Some other creatures also lay eggs. Moths lay eggs on leaves, while a turtle lays its eggs in the warm sand. Crocodiles and some snakes and lizards also lay eggs. Frogs lay eggs in water. Their eggs hatch out into baby frogs which we call tadpoles.

Read this story, then circle the correct answer in each pair.

1. (a) Only some birds lay eggs.
    (b) All birds lay eggs.

2. (a) Only some birds build nests.
    (b) All birds build nests.

3. (a) Birds are the only creatures that lay eggs.
    (b) Some other creatures apart from birds lay eggs.

4. (a) The mother bird pecks on the shell to hatch the children.
    (b) The baby bird pecks on the inside of the shell.

5. (a) Moths lay their eggs on leaves.
    (b) Moths lay their eggs in nests.

6. (a) Baby frogs are called tadpoles.
    (b) Baby frogs are called crocodiles.

7. (a) The yolk of an egg is yellow.
    (b) The yolk of an egg is blue.

8. (a) Some lizards and snakes lay eggs.
    (b) No lizards and snakes lay eggs.

Read the following carefully, then write your answers in the spaces.

Example   The black dog barked loudly at Joanne
as she climbed over the tall fence.

Nouns

1. Which word is the name of an animal?

_____

2. Which word is the name of a person?

_____

Verbs

3. Which word tells us what the dog did?

_____

4. What word tells us what Joanne did?

_____

Adjectives

5. Which word tells us what sort of dog it
   was?

_____

6. Which word tells us what sort of fence it
   was?

_____

Adverbs

7. What word tells us how the dog barked?

_____

8. Which word tells us how Joanne climbed
   the tall fence?

_____

Pronouns

9. What word takes the place of Joanne?

_____

Conjunctions

10. Which word joins the two parts of the
    sentence?

_____

Sentences always begin with a capital letter. Those that are statements end with a full stop.

Example   it is hot today   should be written
             It is hot today.

Underline the sentence in each pair that has the correct punctuation.
Write the other sentence correctly.

1. a bird is in the tree
    The cat is in the cot.

    _____

2. It is nearly lunch time.
    This apple is sour

    _____

3. my friends will be here soon
    John is my best friend.

    _____

4. My uncle lives nearby
    My mother works at the supermarket.

    _____

5. i like to play games.
    She is nine years old.

    _____

6. A spider has eight legs.
    An insect has six legs

    _____

7. She helped me clean the room.
    The city is ten kilometres away

    _____

    _____

8. we played football yesterday
    She saw him at the disco.

    _____

A sentence always begins with a capital letter and, if it is a statement, ends with a full stop. However, we must also remember to use capital letters for proper nouns — the names of people, places, and so on.

Example   *Mr Jones, Paula, Melbourne, England*

Add the capital letters and full stops where they are needed. Write each sentence correctly.

1. my best friend is cathy

   _____

   _____

2. michael is going to england next year

   _____

   _____

3. tom and mary live in sydney

   _____

4. chan and ken both come from vietnam

   _____

   _____

5. when sam was in melbourne he met jack in bourke street

   _____

   _____

6. mrs smith and mr jones returned from canada last week

   _____

   _____

7. tom told us that the city of venice was in italy

   _____

   _____

8. john, peter and effy, who all live in perth, are doing a project on asia

   _____

   _____

   _____

A sentence always begins with a capital letter. However, we also use capital letters to begin the names of people, places, days of the week, months of the year, planets, streets, special times and so on.

Example   *Jack, Newcastle, Tuesday, April, Venice, Wattle Street, Christmas*

Add the capital letters where they are needed in each sentence. Mark them in red.

1. last monday my friend, brian, came to my home.

2. next april paul and I are going to vietnam.

3. george was fishing in the yarra river when he saw sue.

4. the last tuesday in december is christmas day.

5. maggie and martin both live in wattle street in melbourne.

6. andrew and darcy caught the train in spencer street.

7. i was told by alfie last wednesday that the closest planet to the sun is mercury.

8. it is nearly easter and next week it will be good friday.

A question asks something. A question always begins with a capital letter and ends with a question mark.

Example

Where did he go?   Why did you hit him?   (These are questions.)
He is in the kitchen. I hit him because he was silly.   (These are not questions.)

Look at each pair of sentences. Decide which one asks a question. If it is a question, add a question mark. If it is not a question, add a full stop.

1. What colour is a penguin
    It is black and white

2. They grow under the ground
    Where do peanuts grow

3. She is eighteen years old
    How old is your sister

4. When did Jeff arrive
    He arrived at nine o'clock

5. Why did he shoot the fox
    It was eating the chickens

6. How did the prisoner escape
    The door was left open

7. Next Friday is the last school day
    Is this the last day of term

8. What did you do yesterday
    I played netball yesterday

A question always begins with a capital letter and ends with a question mark.

For example,   *Where is the boy going?*

A statement begins with a capital letter and ends with a full stop.

For example,   *The boy is going to Melbourne.*

Look at each pair of sentences.
Add the punctuation needed for each one. Use a red pen.

1.   what is the time
     it is nearly ten o'clock

2.   she will play netball
     what sport is mary playing today

3.   why is the baby crying
     it is crying because it is hungry

4.   is it time for us to go
     we will have to wait five more minutes

5.   who owns that bicycle
     the bicycle belongs to me

6.   when is the bus due
     it should arrive soon

7.   how did jack get the ball down
     he cut off a branch of the tree

8.   in which month is Christmas
     it is in december

9.   i bought it at the canteen
     where did you get that pie

10. it is our turn to empty the bins
     whose job is it to do the bins today

All sentences begin with a capital letter. If the sentence is a statement, it ends in a full stop. If it is a question, it ends with a question mark.

Example

bill has a new bicycle have you seen it
Bill has a new bicycle. Have you seen it?

Add the punctuation needed in each of the following. Use a red pen.

1. i met the new boy have you met him

   _____

   _____

2. i don't like pizza do you like it

   _____

   _____

3. what colour is a penguin it is black and white

   _____

   _____

4. billy is crying loudly do you know why

   _____

   _____

5. how many legs has a spider it has eight legs

   _____

   _____

6. this is rob's new bicycle when did he get it

   _____

   _____

7. my puppy is still missing have you seen it

   _____

   _____

8. we are one short for the team has phil arrived yet

   _____

   _____

9. i can't lift this chair will you help me

   _____

   _____

10. do you remember where i put my glasses i had them only ten minutes ago

    _____

    _____

Remember, all sentences begin with a capital letter and statements end with full stops.

For example,   *It is very cold.*

Questions end with question marks.
For example,   *Is it cold?*

It is important to know how to punctuate statements and questions correctly.

For example,   *he has lost his ball have you seen it*
He has lost his ball. Have you seen it?
                    or
have you seen julie she is in the room
Have you seen Julie? She is in the room.

Add the punctuation needed to the sentences below.

1. michael has a new puppy have you
    seen it

    _____

    _____

2. i have lots to do will you help me

    _____

    _____

3. ian doesn't like david do you like him

    _____

    _____

4. i found this pencil does it belong to you

    _____

    _____

5. i liked that movie did you see it

    _____

    _____

6. what colour is a magpie it is black and
    white

    _____

    _____

7. how many legs has a beetle it has six legs

    _____

    _____

8. what is your favourite food it is pizza

    _____

    _____

9. when is mary's birthday it is in april

    _____

    _____

10. when is christmas day it is in december

    _____

    _____

Commas are used to show pauses in writing, or to separate the words in a list.

For example,   *He put the chisel, hammer, file and screwdriver into the toolbox.*

We also use a comma to separate groups of words.

For example,   *We looked under the table, beside the desk, near the sink, but couldn't find the pencil.*

Add the commas where they are needed in each sentence.

1. The three colours of the Australian flag are red white and blue.

   _____

   _____

2. The planets closest to the sun are Mercury Venus Earth and Mars.

   _____

   _____

3. My favourite foods are apples bananas pizzas and chocolate.

   _____

   _____

4. Flies bees beetles ants and grasshoppers are all insects

   _____

   _____

5. Carly Jack Paul Martin and Annie are the oldest children in our grade.

   _____

   _____

6. Four types of vegetables are potatoes tomatoes lettuces and peas.

   _____

   _____

7. The dog ran along the fence across the road down the steps into the yard and through the front door.

   _____

   _____

8. I helped him sweep the path wash the dishes hang out the clothes clean the fireplace and cut the lawn.

   _____

   _____

Sometimes we join two words to make them shorter. The new word is called a contraction. We use an apostrophe (') to show where we have left out letters.

Example   **do not**   *don't*

Write the contraction for the bold words. Don't forget to put the
apostrophe in the correct place.
The first one has been done for you.

1. Bill **is not** here today.

   _____ **(isn't)** _____

2. I **can not** lift this.

   _____

3. **It is** very cold today.

   _____

4. **We are** leaving shortly.

   _____

5. I don't know **who has** taken the pens.

   _____

6. Luke **was not** feeling very well.

   _____

7. We **did not** know where to go.

   _____

8. I **will not** help you unless you work harder.

   _____

9. He said **you will** have to do it yourself.

   _____

10. **We have** looked everywhere but cannot find it.

    _____

GRAMMAR IN OUR LANGUAGE
PUNCTUATION TEST CHECK

Use a red pen to add the punctuation needed in each sentence.
Write each sentence correctly.

Example

we saw tom in melbourne last tuesday
We saw Tom in Melbourne last Tuesday.

1. my best friends are joe and robyn

   _____

   _____

2. when are you going to england

   _____

   _____

3. last tuesday mr smith took sharon to perth

   _____

   _____

4. is john's birthday in april or june

   _____

   _____

5. last thursday sam went fishing in the murray river with jock and toni

   _____

   _____

   _____

6. con has lost his new pencil case have you seen it

   _____

   _____

7. josh planted carrots peas beans potatoes and tomatoes in the garden

   _____

   _____

8. daniel looked under the table on top of the chair near the television and in the bedroom but could not find his knife

   _____

   _____

   _____

[ ] denotes the unit to refer to.

1. Which word is the name of something?
   An axeman cut down the large tree.
   (a) cut   (b) down   (d) tree   **[1]**

2. Choose the word that best fills the gap.
   A large _____ of fish was in the bay.
   (a) swam   (b) school   (c) fleet   **[2]**

3. Which two words should begin with a
   capital letter?
   september   table   light
   tree   paul   fruit   **[3]**

4. Make this word mean more than one.
   one dish   seven _____   **[4]**

5. Make this word mean more than one.
   one city   two _____   **[5]**

6. Make this word mean more than one.
   one knife   three _____   **[6]**

7. Which word tells us what Cathy did?
   Cathy climbed a tree last night.
   (a) tree   (b) climbed   (c) night   **[7]**

8. Add *-ing* to the word in brackets and write it
   in the space.
   I am _____ all the lollies. (take)   **[8]**

9. Write the word in brackets in its correct form
   in the space.
   I _____ at the corner yesterday.
   (stop)   **[9]**

10. Choose the correct word to fill the space.
    Bill and I _____ to play netball.
    (likes   like)   **[10]**

11. Choose the correct word to fill the space.
    The girls _____ here.
    (was   were)   **[11]**

12. Which word takes the place of Nathan?
    One day Nathan was playing golf when he
    saw a friend riding a bike.
    (a) she   (b) he   (c) friend   **[12]**

13. Which word best fills the gap?
    She is diving _____ the water.
    (a) into   (b) above   (c) inside   **[13]**

14. What word tells us when Tom came?
    Tom came to our home yesterday.
    (a) came   (b) yesterday   (c) home   **[14]**

15. What word best describes the dog?
    The large dog barked savagely.
    (a) large   (b) barked   (c) savagely   **[15]**

16. What word best fills the space?
    We must leave _____ it begins to rain.
    (a) beside   (b) when   (c) but   **[16]**

17. Which of these is a complete sentence?
    (a) When it was cold.
    (b) The girls played in the rain.
    (c) Bird nest sat the on.   **[17,18,19]**

18. Punctuate the sentence.
    my friend mel went to melbourne last
    thursday _____

    _____ **[21,22,23]**

19. Punctuate this sentence.
    where did john go

    _____ **[24, 25, 26, 27]**

20. Add the missing commas.
    I ate pies chips apples pears and lollies for
    lunch.   **[28]**

21. Write the bold word as two words.
    I **mustn't** be late for school.

    _____ _____ **[29]**